**May 16, 1969**—"I'm going to die here."
That's what Private Mike Serrano
thought as he lay in the mud. He was
surrounded by dead soldiers and covered
in blood.

## The Mission

Serrano and his unit were in the middle of one of the bloodiest battles of the Vietnam War. Their mission was to take Hill 937 from their enemy, the North Vietnamese Army (NVA).

To U.S. soldiers, Hill 937 had another name. They called it Hamburger Hill— because soldiers were ground up there like in a meat grinder.

## Death Trap

The NVA had turned Hamburger Hill into a giant death trap. Armed with grenade launchers and machine guns, NVA soldiers waited in the trees and hid in holes in the ground. Patches on their uniforms read "kill Americans."

"There was a feeling of evil there. A feeling of doom," Serrano remembers.

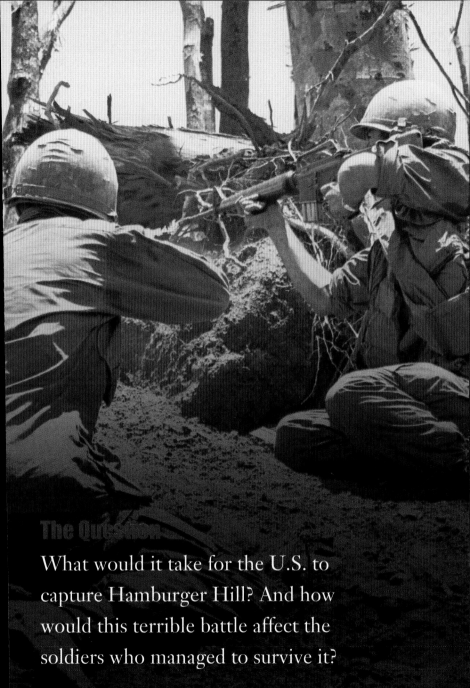

What would it take for the U.S. to capture Hamburger Hill? And how would this terrible battle affect the soldiers who managed to survive it?

## PREVIEW PHOTOS

**PAGE 1: A wounded paratrooper from the 101st Airborne Division lies on Hamburger Hill.**

**PAGES 2-3: Soldiers charge up Hamburger Hill.**

**PAGES 4-5: U.S. soldiers fire into an NVA bunker near the top of Hamburger Hill.**

**Cover design:** Maria Bergós, Book&Look **Interior design:** Red Herring Design/NYC **Photo Credits** ©: cover top: sculpies/Shutterstock; cover bottom: Larry Burrows/The LIFE Picture Collection/Getty Images; 1: Bettmann/Getty Images; 2-3: Bettmann/Getty Images; 4-5: Bettmann/Getty Images; 8: Hulton Archive/Getty Images; 10: From the personal collection of Mike Serrano; 12: From the personal collection of Mike Serrano; 13: Bettmann/Getty Images; 15 top: Charles Bonnay, 1968/Stockphoto.com/Black Star; 15 bottom: stf/AP Images; 16: Stockphoto.com/Black Star; 18: Moviestore Collection, Ltd./Alamy Images; 19: David Lindroth, Inc.; 20: AP Images; 21: Tim Page/Corbis/Getty Images; 22: akg-images; 24: La Porte County Historical Society Museum; 26: Ray Cranbourne, 1968/Stockphoto.com/Black Star; 28: AP Images; 29: Vietnam-Gear.com; 30 left: Vincent Giordano Photo/Shutterstock; 30 center: Corbis/Getty Images; 30 right: Corbis/Getty Images; 31 left: Richard Strauss/National Museum of American History, Smithsonian Institution; 31 center top: AP Images; 31 center bottom: The Art Archive/Shutterstock; 31 right: Ed Darack/Superstock, Inc.; 32: Henri Huet/AP Images; 34: Bettmann/Getty Images; 35: Hugh Van Es/AP Images; 36: From the personal collection of Arthur Wiknik Jr.; 38-39: Rolls Press/Popperfoto/Getty Images; 40: From the personal collection of Mike Serrano; 41: Nathan Benn; 42 top: Bettmann/Getty Images; 42 center: Bettmann/Getty Images; 42 bottom left: ullstein bild/The Granger Collection; 42 bottom right: The Granger Collection; 43 top left: John Filo/Getty Images; 43 top right: Bettmann/Getty Images; 43 bottom left: Bettmann/Getty Images; 43 bottom right: ADN-Bildarchiv/ullstein bild/Getty Image; 44: AP Images; 45: The Art Archive/Shutterstock.

Library of Congress Cataloging-in-Publication Data
Names: DiConsiglio, John, author.
Title: Three days in Vietnam : a vet's harrowing story / John DiConsiglio.
Other titles: Xbooks.
Description: [New edition] | New York, NY : Scholastic, [2020]. |
Series: Xbooks | Includes index. | Audience: Grades 4-6 | Summary: "Book about the three days in Vietnam"-- Provided by publisher.
Identifiers: LCCN 2019029898 | ISBN 9780531238172 (library binding) | ISBN 9780531243831 (paperback)
Subjects: LCSH: Serrano, Mike--Juvenile literature. | Soldiers--United States--Biography--Juvenile literature. | Hamburger Hill, Battle of, Vietnam, 1969--Juvenile literature. | Vietnam War, 1961-1975--Campaigns--Juvenile literature.
Classification: LCC DS557.8.A54 D525 2020 | DDC 959.704/342--dc23

Printed in Johor Bahru, Malaysia    108

SCHOLASTIC, XBOOKS, and associated logos are trademarks and/or registered trademarks of Scholastic Inc.

1  2  3  4  5  6  7  8  9  10  R  29  28  27  26  25  24  23  22  21  20

Scholastic Inc., 557 Broadway, New York, NY 10012.

# THREE DAYS IN
# VIETNAM

## A Vet's Harrowing Story

JOHN DiCONSIGLIO

SCHOLASTIC

**THIS U.S. SOLDIER** of the 173rd Airborne Brigade has just received a fresh supply of ammunition and water. He was on a jungle "search and destroy" patrol in Vietnam.

# TABLE OF CONTENTS

**MIKE SERRANO** (center) with two of his buddies a month before the battle at Hamburger Hill

# 1

# Into the Killing Zone

**A U.S. soldier is sent into
a fierce battle on Hill 937.**

*Mike Serrano had been in Vietnam for six months when
his battalion was sent to Hill 937, known as Hamburger Hill.
The hill was in the A Shau Valley, a dangerous hideout for
the North Vietnamese Army (NVA). Here is Serrano's story.*

In May 1969, I was on a three-day [leave] at
Vietnam's China Beach. It was a coastal resort on the
South China Sea where American soldiers went to
surf and take a break from the war. I was hanging out

# Private Mike Serrano

**HOMETOWN:** San Leandro, CA
**AGE WHEN DRAFTED:** 19
**RANK:** Private
**UNIT:** 1st Battalion, 506th Regiment, 101st Airborne
**ARRIVED IN VIETNAM:** November 1968

**More than half a million Americans fought in the Vietnam War. Mike Serrano was one of them.**

When Mike Serrano graduated from high school in 1966, he knew it wouldn't be long before he'd be drafted into the army and sent to Vietnam.

During the Vietnam War, the U.S. government used a lottery system to fill the ranks of the armed services. This system was known as the draft. Several of Serrano's friends had already been drafted. They'd received a government form letter that ordered them to report for duty.

Serrano got his letter in March 1968. He didn't know what to expect when he got to Vietnam. His friends who'd returned from the war didn't want to talk about it.

Still, at 19, Serrano wasn't scared of going to war. To him, it was as much a part of growing up as getting his driver's license. His father and uncles had fought in World War II. "I felt it was my turn now," he recalls. "It was like some big John Wayne adventure."

with an old high school buddy. I had such a good time that I almost missed the helicopter back to my unit.

When I returned, my friend Chuck Page said he was sorry to see me. He was hoping I'd miss that chopper. We were going on a mission, he said. And it didn't sound good. [Another unit] was engaged in a fierce fight with a strong NVA force on Hill 937. We were supposed to be their reinforcements.

**THE A SHAU VALLEY** was a training ground for NVA soldiers. The NVA also used the valley to smuggle weapons from North Vietnam to communist fighters in South Vietnam.

My battalion had patrolled the A Shau Valley since early spring. It was a place of malevolent beauty. Some of it was lush and green and as pretty as a postcard. But there was also this eerie feeling in the valley. We had a Vietnamese scout who was terrified by it. "Very bad," he warned us. "*Beaucoup* [many] killers." He ran away rather than go into that valley. But soldiers don't think about the dangers—or at least they don't talk about it. Soldiers adapted to the Vietnam jungles. You had to if you wanted to survive.

## Misery in the Jungle

You got very little sleep. It was horribly hot; you were always dripping with sweat. Most of the time you ate out of cans. When you were in the field, you were lucky if you took a shower once a month. You were more concerned about keeping your socks dry than about the enemy.

It didn't take long for us to figure out that all we really wanted was for us and our buddies to be safe.

# The Vietnam War

## Here are some FAQs about the war in Vietnam.

**When did the conflict in Vietnam begin?**
The answer goes back at least as far as 1954. At that time, Vietnam was split into two parts—North Vietnam and South Vietnam.

**What was the conflict between North and South Vietnam?**

Ho Chi Minh

The leader of North Vietnam, Ho Chi Minh, made the country communist. That's a system in which one all-powerful political party controls its citizens' economic and political lives. South Vietnam was not communist—but Ho Chi Minh wanted it to be. He planned to take it over and make it part of a united, all-communist Vietnam.

**Why was the United States interested in this dispute?**
The U.S. was opposed to the spread of communism. It feared that if South Vietnam fell to the communists, neighboring countries would, too. Laos, Cambodia, and Thailand would fall like "dominoes."

**Why did the United States get involved?**
The U.S. promised to help any country threatened by a communist takeover. So when communist rebels began raids in South Vietnam, the U.S. stepped in. The U.S. sent military advisers and economic aid to help South Vietnam.

**When did U.S. soldiers arrive in Vietnam?**

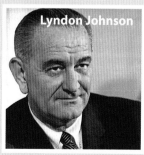
Lyndon Johnson

In 1964, U.S. president Lyndon Johnson asked Congress to give him the power to "take all necessary steps, including the use of armed forces" to help South Vietnam.

And so began a war that would last more than ten years—and cost millions of lives.

**A U.S. SOLDIER** stays low as he advances toward an enemy position in Vietnam.

# 2

# Up the Hill

**On May 14, Serrano's platoon
joins the battle on Hamburger Hill.**

We were led by Sergeant Roger Pedue. Roger stuck
out in our camp. The platoon was mostly 18-year-old
kids from big cities like New York and Los Angeles.
Roger was a lanky blond farm boy from Indiana. At
26, he was an old man to us. We teased him for being
a "lifer"—a career military man. All he ever wanted to
be was a soldier. But we trusted Roger with our lives.
He was like a mother hen, making sure we were safe.

On May 14, we started up the hill. We heard gunfire and air strikes. The battle was well underway.

We weren't a quarter of the way to the top of the hill before we were attacked. I didn't even see the enemy. They jumped out of these deeply dug bunkers and fired at us from every angle. The noise was deafening.

The fighting was so bad that helicopters couldn't land to resupply our ammo. They hovered overhead and kicked guns down to us on the ground.

**U.S. TROOPS** fight their way up the hill in this scene from the 1987 film *Hamburger Hill*.

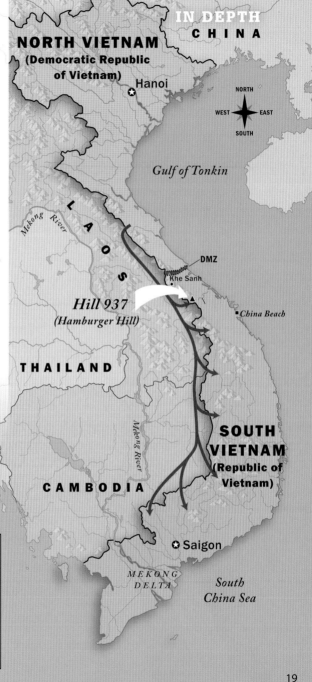

# Vietnam

During the Vietnam War, the U.S. fought with South Vietnam against the North. Hill 937, known as Hamburger Hill, was in South Vietnam, in the A Shau Valley. The Ho Chi Minh Trail ran through the valley. The North Vietnamese used the trail to move troops and weapons into South Vietnam.

**NORTH VIETNAM** (Democratic Republic of Vietnam)

Hanoi

CHINA

*Gulf of Tonkin*

L A O S

*Mekong River*

DMZ

Khe Sanh

*Hill 937* (Hamburger Hill)

China Beach

THAILAND

*Mekong River*

**SOUTH VIETNAM** (Republic of Vietnam)

CAMBODIA

*Gulf of Thailand*

Saigon

*MEKONG DELTA*

*South China Sea*

NORTH
WEST — EAST
SOUTH

**KEY**
- North Vietnam
- South Vietnam
- DMZ (demilitarized zone)
- Ho Chi Minh Trail
- national capital

| 0 | 100 mi. |
| 0 | 100 km |

19

We fought all day on the 14th. On the 15th, we got a little higher up the hill—maybe a third of the way up. But we took heavy casualties from NVA ambushes. They weren't going to let us up that hill—no ifs, ands, or buts. We clawed for every inch of ground.

## An Easy Target

We set up camp on the night of the 15th. I heard tree branches rustling in the dark. The NVA were moving around us, digging in for the morning attacks.

Our radio operator had been killed, and I was picked to take his place. I wasn't sure if I wanted to. Everyone knew the enemy aimed for the guy with the radio on his back. I'd be an easy target.

But the radio guy also got first pick of candy and cigarettes. I decided it was worth it.

**RADIO OPERATORS** kept platoon leaders in touch with their commanders.

**A TRANSPORT HELICOPTER**
delivers troops to a battle zone
while soldiers in a trench get
instructions from a commander.

# 3

# The Point Man

**On May 16, NVA soldiers are poised to attack Serrano's platoon.**

At dawn, Roger [Pedue] walked by as I was strapping on the radio. At first, he didn't say anything. He reached into his pocket and pulled out a pack of cigarettes. He lit one and handed the rest to me. Then he calmly told me that our platoon would lead the attack.

There was silence between us. Roger looked me in the eyes. "You know, they're waiting for us, Mike," he said. I nodded. The NVA were planning an ambush. The point man in our unit—the soldier in the lead—would be as good as dead.

Roger blew smoke into the air. Our squad was a

bunch of guys who hadn't been in Vietnam long. There were only two men experienced enough to walk point, Roger said. "Me and you." He stomped his cigarette under his boot and gave me a cockeyed grin. "And I'm better at it than you," he smiled. "Besides, we can't afford to lose the radio."

I realized what he was saying. Roger knew he was going to die.

# Military Units

This chart shows how U.S. military units were generally organized during the Vietnam War.

| UNIT | LEADER | |
| --- | --- | --- |
| **squad** | Sergeant | |
| **platoon** | Lieutenant | |
| **company** | Captain | |
| **battalion** | Lieutenant colonel | |
| **brigade/ regiment** | Colonel | |
| **division** | Major general | ★★ |

# Saying Good-bye

Roger rarely talked about himself. But as we stood there, he told me about a girl back in Indiana. He was in love with her. She had two children, and he cared for them like they were his own. "If I ever get out of this, Mike," he said, "I'm gonna ask that girl to marry me."

It was almost time for the company to move out. Roger told me to take care of the men. My heart was racing. He was saying good-bye.

I could have volunteered to walk point. But the words wouldn't come out. I just said, "Roger, don't be a hero."

He smiled and walked away.

| SIZE | FYI |
|------|-----|
| **4–10 soldiers** (also called troops) | A squad was the smallest fighting unit in the army. |
| **About 16–40 soldiers** (3–4 squads) | Platoons included riflemen, machine gunners, radio operators, and other specialists. |
| **100–200 soldiers** (3–4 platoons) | The size of a company depended on its mission. |
| **500–1,000 soldiers** (3–5 companies) | A battalion was capable of undertaking an independent combat mission. |
| **3,000–5,000 soldiers** (3 or more battalions) | Some brigades were led by a brigadier general. |
| **10,000–18,000 soldiers** (3 brigades/regiments) | A division was big enough to conduct a major military operation. |

**U.S. TROOPS** patrol a jungle in Vietnam. The thick undergrowth provided plenty of hiding places for NVA soldiers.

# 4

# Ambushed

**Roger Pedue gives his life
to save the men in his platoon.**

A few minutes later, we started up the hill. Roger was on point. We were no more than 150 feet out when Roger stopped in the trail. Suddenly, he sprayed gunfire into the trees. That's when all hell broke loose.

It was an ambush. Roger must have seen something. Rather than have us walk into a shooting gallery, he sprung the trap. NVA soldiers popped out of spider holes. [Those are small hiding places dug into the ground.] They dropped from trees.

**U.S. SOLDIERS TRY TO HELP** a badly wounded comrade during the battle at Hamburger Hill.

Roger was hit first. He rolled off the trail.

He could have laid there quietly until a medic got to him. Instead, he tossed grenades at the enemy. The NVA aimed all of their firepower at him. That gave the rest of us time to move into position. But Roger was struck with round after round. He never had a chance.

I crawled to one side of the trail and tried to work the radio. It was busted.

Then my M-16 rifle jammed. I was a sitting duck.

# Hit!

A rocket grenade exploded next to me. Shrapnel—sharp metal fragments—pierced my right arm and leg. My left foot was bleeding bad. I could feel my right side going numb when my friend Chuck somehow found me. He yelled at me to hold on for a medic. Then he looked at my back.

"Oh my god, Mike," he gasped. A hail of shrapnel had ripped the radio on my back apart—but it stopped the shrapnel. That radio saved my life.

**A RADIO** like this shielded Mike Serrano's back from shrapnel—and saved his life.

# Weapons of War

In the dense jungles of Vietnam, firefights could erupt at any time. Troops needed lightweight weapons that were reliable—and deadly. Here's a look at some of the weapons used by the two sides during the Vietnam War.

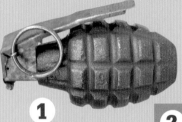

## UNITED STATES AND SOUTH VIETNAM

### 1 MARK 2 GRENADES

A soldier could throw one of these grenades 30 yards.

An explosive inside the grenade shattered the metal casing. The explosion sent metal fragments, or shrapnel, flying. A Mark 2 was deadly within 15 yards of where it landed.

### 2 M-79 GRENADE LAUNCHER

Known as the "Thumper," the M-79 looked like a sawed-off shotgun. It could accurately fire grenades, smoke bombs, and flares to nearly 700 feet.

### 3 M-60 MACHINE GUN

This lightweight weapon took two soldiers to operate— a gunner and an assistant. The gun was fired from a three-legged stand called a tripod. Or it was attached to tanks or helicopters. It had a range of 1,900 yards. And it had a maximum firing rate of 550 rounds per minute.

## NORTH VIETNAM AND VIET CONG

### 4 M-16 RIFLE

Most U.S. troops carried short, light M-16s. The version used in the early years of the war jammed easily and was hard to keep clean in the field. An improved version was later developed. The M-16's bullets were held in metal clips, or magazines, that popped into the rifle.

### 5 RPG-2 ROCKET LAUNCHER

This lightweight weapon was held on the shoulder. It fired a rocket-propelled grenade (RPG) that exploded on impact. It was used against armored vehicles, enemy forts, and helicopters. It was eventually replaced by the more accurate RPG-7.

### 6 AK-47 ASSAULT RIFLE

Also known as the Kalashnikov. Heavier and less accurate than the M-16, this gun's solid frame made it more durable in the jungle.

### 7 81-MM MORTAR

This short, portable cannon could fire a 15-inch rocket the length of a football field. It took a crew of three to carry the bulky weapon.

**A MEDIC TREATS** a U.S. soldier who had been wounded in an ambush by the Viet Cong.

# 5

# "It Could Have Been Me"

**Serrano is badly wounded on Hamburger Hill. But at least he's alive.**

I barely remember being carried off the hill. Someone dragged me back to the perimeter with the wounded and the dead. A medic screamed that a MedEvac chopper was on its way.

The guy lying next to me had half his leg shot off. I could see the bone protruding from his knee. I heard constant gunfire from the hill.

That's when it started raining. Waves of water fell over me in sheets, washing the blood down my arms and legs. I was soaking wet and shivering. I remember thinking, *I'm never getting off this hill. I'm going to die here.*

## Losing a Friend

I looked over at a row of dead bodies in the clearing. They were covered in plastic ponchos. The rain beat down on them. The wind blew a poncho aside and I saw a soldier's bloody leg. Someone told me it was Roger.

I sat there in the rain looking at Roger. I could hear the MedEvac chopper blades coming closer. The medic yelled at me to hold on. I stared at Roger's body. It could have been me under that poncho.

I shook my head. Why did Roger die? Why did I live?

**A WOUNDED U.S. SOLDIER** **in the A Shau Valley is supported by a fellow soldier.**

WEARY U.S. SOLDIERS rest while on patrol in Vietnam.

**DAZED U.S. SOLDIERS** stand at the top of Hamburger Hill after the battle.

# 6

# After Hamburger Hill

**The battle—and the war—
eventually come to a bloody end.**

Four days after Mike Serrano was evacuated, U.S. soldiers finally reached the top of Hamburger Hill. But less than a month later, U.S. troops left the hill. The goal of the assault had been to kill enemy soldiers, not seize territory. Within days, new NVA forces moved in.

Almost 450 U.S. troops were killed or wounded on Hamburger Hill. After all that bloodshed, most Americans back home had run out of patience with the Vietnam War. They wanted it over—as soon as possible. Antiwar protests were becoming more frequent—and violent. And morale was low among the troops in Vietnam. Finally, in June 1969, the U.S. Army slowly started to withdraw from combat.

## The War Is Over

On January 27, 1973, all sides agreed to a cease-fire. The last U.S. troops flew out of Vietnam two months later. They left behind a weakened South Vietnam. By

1974, its government had collapsed. On April 30, 1975, NVA troops overran Saigon, the capital of South Vietnam. That same day, the country surrendered to the North.

The Vietnam War was over. Nearly 60,000 U.S. soldiers—and more than three million Vietnamese—had been killed. After returning home, many Vietnam veterans remained haunted by their experience. It would take decades for the United States to heal from the wounds of the Vietnam War. **X**

**SHOWN BELOW** are antiwar protestors in Washington, D.C. in 1967.

# Aftermath

**For Serrano, surviving Hamburger Hill was just the beginning of a long struggle.**

Mike Serrano was airlifted off Hamburger Hill. He underwent several surgeries, but he still has shrapnel in his arm and legs.

He returned home in November 1969. But he couldn't leave thoughts of the battle behind. He was angry and depressed until he met the woman who would become his wife. "She was the first person who ever asked me, 'What happened to you over there?'" he recalls. "I broke down crying. I told her the whole story."

Serrano was haunted by Roger Pedue's death. After 20 years, he tracked down Pedue's brother in Indiana. Serrano told him that Pedue had died a hero. And Serrano asked for forgiveness. "I lived with guilt for so long," he says. "Finally I could start healing."

**X FILES**

# Timeline: The Vietnam War

**1954:** France withdraws from Vietnam, which it had ruled as a colony for 100 years. North Vietnam establishes a communist government, while South Vietnam is noncommunist.

**1965:** More than 200,000 U.S. troops are fighting in Vietnam. They're supported by massive aerial bombing.

**1954**   **1961**   **1964**   **1965**   **1968**

**1961:** To aid South Vietnam against communist attacks, the U.S. increases its military and economic support. By 1963, 16,000 American military advisers are in Vietnam.

**1964:** Congress approves President Lyndon Johnson's request to use armed forces to help South Vietnam.

**1968:** The NVA and the Viet Cong (communist rebels in South Vietnam) launch the Tet Offensive. They make more than 100 surprise attacks on targets throughout South Vietnam.

U.S. soldiers kill 500 civilians in the town of My Lai. The massacre shocks the American public.

**1970:** During an antiwar protest at Kent State University in Ohio, National Guardsmen fire into a crowd of protesters. Four students are killed.

**1973:** With many Americans now against the war, President Richard Nixon vows to bring "peace with honor" to Vietnam.

The Paris Peace Accords produce a cease-fire. Two months later, the last U.S. troops withdraw from Vietnam.

**1969**   **1970**   **1972**   **1973**   **1975**

**1969:** 1,800 U.S. troops battle to capture Hamburger Hill. Within weeks, they abandon the hill, and the NVA re-establishes control of the area.

**1972:** With American troops leaving, the North Vietnamese attack a weakened South Vietnam in the Easter Offensive.

**1975:** North Vietnamese troops overrun Saigon, the capital of South Vietnam. The South surrenders, ending the war. Months later, Vietnam unifies as a communist country, the Socialist Republic of Vietnam.

During the Vietnam War, helicopters like the UH-1 Huey and the CH-47 Chinook were used for a variety of purposes.

## MEDICAL EVACUATION

MedEvac "air ambulances" such as the Huey airlifted wounded soldiers to hospitals at nearby military bases. Some soldiers received treatment within 30 minutes of being injured. Thanks to MedEvacs, 81% of soldiers wounded in Vietnam survived, compared to 71% in World War II.

## AIRBORNE ASSAULT

Armor-plated gunships known as "Cobras" or "Hogs" supported ground troops by attacking enemy positions from the air. They were equipped with machine guns, grenade launchers, and rocket launchers.

**UH-1 Huey**

**CH-47 Chinook**

### TROOP TRANSPORT

Transport helicopters such as the Chinook airlifted troops in and out of the jungle. During a major battle, hundreds of choppers—each carrying up to 32 soldiers—could be called into action. "Door gunners" firing machine guns from the helicopters' open doors provided some protection from enemy fire.

### SEARCH AND RESCUE

When pilots were shot down, or when ground troops were separated from their units, helicopters like the Sikorsky CH-3C Jolly Green Giant were sent to find and rescue them. They carried 250-foot cables so they could pull troops out of thick jungles.

### MOVING EQUIPMENT

Big helicopters carried artillery guns and other heavy equipment to distant combat zones. The CH-54 Tarhe was large enough to airlift damaged helicopters.

# RESOURCES

Here's a selection of books for more information about the Vietnam War.

## What to Read Next

### NONFICTION

Freedman, Russell. *Vietnam: A History of the War*. New York: Scholastic, 2016.

O'Connor, Jim. *What Was the Vietnam War?* New York: Penguin Workshop, 2019.

Otfinoski, Steven. *The Vietnam War* (A Step into History). New York: Scholastic Children's Press, 2017.

Partridge, Elizabeth. *Boots on the Ground: America's War in Vietnam*. New York: Viking, 2018.

Townley, Alvin. *Captured: An American Prisoner of War in North Vietnam*. New York: Scholastic, 2019.

*Vietnam War: Discover the People, Places, Battles, and Weapons of America's Indochina Struggle* (DK Eyewitness Books). New York: DK Children, 2017.

Zullo, Allan. *Vietnam War Heroes* (Ten True Tales). New York: Scholastic, 2015.

### FICTION

Burg, Ann E. *All the Broken Pieces*. New York: Scholastic, 2012.

Dowell, Frances O'Roark. *Shooting the Moon*. New York: Atheneum Books, 2010.

Hoppey, Tim. *Jungle Scout: A Vietnam War Story*. North Mankato, Minnesota: Stone Arch Books, 2008.

Hughes, Dean. *Search and Destroy*. New York: Atheneum Books, 2015.

Lynch, Chris. *I Pledge Allegiance* (Vietnam #1). New York: Scholastic, 2011.

Partridge, Elizabeth. *Dogtag Summer*. New York: Bloomsbury Books, 2011.

Watkins, Steve. *On Blood Road*. New York: Scholastic, 2018.

# GLOSSARY

**ambush** (AM-bush) *noun* a sudden surprise attack

**artillery** (ar-TIL-uh-ree) *noun* large, powerful guns, usually mounted on wheels or tracks

**assault** (uh-SAWLT) *noun* a military attack or raid

**casualty** (KAZH-oo-uhl-tee) *noun* a military person killed, wounded, or captured during a battle

**cease-fire** (SEESS-FIRE) *noun* a period during a war when both sides agree to stop fighting

**chopper** (CHOP-uhr) *noun* a slang word for helicopter

**communism** (KOM-yuh-niz-uhm) *noun* a way of organizing a country so that all the land, houses, factories, etc., belong to the government or community, and the resources are shared by all

**demilitarized zone** (DMZ) (dee-MIL-ih-tur-ized ZONE) *noun* during war, a neutral area where military activity is not permitted

**draft** (DRAFT) *noun* a system for selecting individuals from a group for required military service

**evacuate** (ih-VAK-yoo-ate) *verb* to remove or be removed from a dangerous area

**grenade** (gruh-NADE) *noun* a small bomb thrown by hand or fired from a rifle

**harrowing** (HAIR-oh-ing) *adjective* extremely distressing

**magazine** (MAG-uh-zeen) *noun* a container that holds bullets and feeds them into a gun

**malevolent** (muh-LEH-vuh-lint) *adjective* having or indicating a wish to do evil to others

**MedEvac** (MED-ih-vack) *noun* a helicopter used for emergency evacuation of the wounded from a combat area

**medic** (MED-ik) *noun* a person trained to give medical help during a battle

**mortar** (MOR-tur) *noun* a very short cannon that fires shells or rockets high in the air

**North Vietnamese Army** (NVA) (NORTH vee-et-nuh-MEEZ ARM-ee) *noun* the armed forces of North Vietnam

**perimeter** (puh-RIM-uh-tur) *noun* the defended border of a military position

**protruding** (pro-TROO-ding) *adjective* sticking out

**reinforcements** (ree-in-FORSS-muhnts) *noun* extra troops sent to strengthen a fighting force

**rocket-propelled grenade** (ROK-it pruh-PELD gruh-NADE) *noun* a hand-held, shoulder-launched weapon that fires grenades

**shrapnel** (SHRAP-nuhl) *noun* small pieces of metal scattered by an exploding shell or bomb

# INDEX

## Metric Conversions

**Feet to meters:** 1 ft is about 0.3 m
**Miles to kilometers:** 1 mi is about 1.6 km
**Pounds to kilograms:** 1 lb is about 0.45 kg
**Ounces to grams:** 1 oz is about 28 g